T0270013

THE FULL MEASURE

Poems from *The Full Measure* have been published in *Aethlon, Ascent Aspirations, Between the Lines, Cyclamen & Swords* (April and December), *Connotation Press* Issue v, Volume ii, *CV2, Descant, Great Lakes Journal, Humanist Perspectives, The Lynn River Review* Volume 2, *Lummox, Morel, Numéro Cinq, Open Hearts, Poemata, Port Dover Maple Leaf, Quills, Raddle Moon, Vallum, Voices Israel, Windsor Review*, and in the anthologies *Beyond the Seventh Morning, Family Ties, Food for Thought, Lemon Tradewinds, Pith and Wry, Place of Places, Spirit Eyes and Fireflies, The Poet's Quest for God, Ultra Best Short Verse, and Under the Weight of Heaven.*

Two poems from *The Full Measure* were selected as being the inaugural feature in Morel's *Featured Poet* series.

Poems from *The Full Measure* have received First Place in the *Ascent Aspirations* poetry prize, Judge's Choice Award in *Food for Thought*, Honourable Mention in the *Open Hearts* poetry prize and *Poemata's Canadian Poetry Association* annual poetry prize, Runner-Up in the *Ontario Poetry Society's* Ultra Short Poetry Prize, and the winner of the Winston Collins/Descant Prize for Best Canadian Poem of 2013.

The Full Measure

John B. Lee

Black Moss Press
2015

Library and Archives Canada Cataloguing in Publication

Lee, John B., 1951-, author
    The full measure / John B. Lee.

Poems.
ISBN 978-0-88753-550-5 (paperback)

I. Title.

PS8573.E348F84 2015   C811'.54   C2015-903874-X

Cover photo by Marty Gervais
Layout & design by Jay Rankin
Edited by Meghan Desjardins

Published by Black Moss Press at 2450 Byng Road, Windsor, Ontario, N8W 3E8. Canada. Black Moss books are distributed in Canada and the U.S. by Fitzhenry & Whiteside. All orders should be directed there.

Fitzhenry & Whiteside
195 Allstate Parkway
Markham, ON
L3R 4T8

Black Moss would like to acknowledge the generous financial support from both the Canada Council for the Arts and the Ontario Arts Council.

CONTENTS

TODAY I AM REMEMBERING

how I came to work in the garden after the rain
where weed greened the earth
at the end of the row
lambsquarters and pigweed
thrilled the headlands
and thickened the hill
with the wild energy of twitch and thistle
ditches blooming with bloodroot near school
drowning the strong scent of wet land
whitened by lace and the cruel itch that nettled the fencerow
and in the corn the soft-leafed lactation of bitter-milk
leaked from the hoe-broken stalk
its creased pod otherwise pillowed with seed kites
would split the seams
at the end of summer
and everything unbuttoned its orange-winged blouse
to the berry cane and the thorn
and the sparrows were singing
between the pockets
about long-branched loblolly
in the muck-thirsty sun
what nests there
thatched their bowl in the first morning
when my lost cousin came to the farm
a catkin divining his palm line
dowsing the willow that witched the well
beneath a blue-grey sky blushed with a bow
blessing the shape of all seen things
fading to a covenant's damp caress of warm light
arcing over the farouche and wave-shocked shore
where I live on the lake

my body cup-circled by darkness
like driftwood shadowed by dream
and though I was once time's sweet darling
now   I am
remembering more   imagining less

A BOY AND HIS DOG

it all but breaks my heart to recall
myself as a sentimental boy
on the first day of his first dog
living what would be a five-dog life
when Tip was a fat English Collie pup
leaping my lap

he had been born
in my grandfather's barn
whelped in the straw
and weaned in the cold
in the half-dark of the Mull farm road
from whence he came to us
plump and six weeks old

and in my favourite childhood photograph
he is climbing my shirt
to the last button
licking my face and wagging his weight
in my arms
and I am loved by that
jubilant worming of spine
that comes
when a dog brings joy
to a child's unbroken embrace

hard to forgive
eaten by time
and the damp of the house
how that image
was stolen by circles of spore that rotted the mat
as memory lost its last proof
like the melting of snow in late spring

hard to forget
how he lay on the hill
at the end of the day
watching the line
to mark our
returning from school

and I beg the master
of each dark and unresponsive night
may all most serious stars
that roam past calling
hear me
with the wishing
and quietest whisper of prayer
come home and come home and
come home

THE BOY WITH THE BOOK ON HIS HEAD

my mother was teaching her daughter
the elegant posture of girls
though my sister walked
with a sway in her spine
mother said—straighten your back
to the door
and I'll measure your worth
with a mark
for your height and your growth in the day

and she placed on the round
of her hair
a copy of thought
and said, walk without spilling the words
as if she were
come from a well
with a jug of old sky
to sweeten the thirst of her home
with a portable potable blue
and it spilled
like the flight of a bird
its fluttering pages
like wings
as it breathed to the floor
with a thump
and a clop that went red
for its covers were red
an unreadable red
like the unwanted blushing of love
or the blood of our Lord
in the wine

and so I said
mother, miter me with
that sensible hat

and she set me the task
and I strode
and was straight in my care
like those who suffer from aches in their bones
or those who
are old on the ice

and I felt myself
crowned by a book
and I danced on the floor
like the dream of a dog
and I flickered like feathers in flame

but what of my sister
poor girl
she caught my cool shadow
in play
like the darkness of shadow in shade

and what might I say
that I'm sorry
for being
the boy with the book on his head

I'll just
sit in the corner and *be*

THE BUZZ OF VOICES

my sister playing hopscotch
by the scalding shed
finding all she needs so close at hand
she needs nothing but hands
a chalk and a stone
and a place to stand
outlining the court
with the white drag
of a calcified rock
found in the yard
with a flat pebble for tossing
and then
it's one foot one foot
two foot one ...
count and turn
stagger where you lean
retrieving glory like the lame girl
from another story
heaven's blue theatre making her
its brief marionette
the wing shadow of her balance-keeping arm
staining the thin grass and darkened gravel
as she dances alone
in the memory of evening after supper
on the farm
even the gate-creak gone
even the willow
the broad-hipped melancholia of its
whisper of green wind
gone, even the
heavy-boned branches of the old apple

lost in the mind
along with the dung-dappled
sheep-pelleted lawn
littered like some battle-blackened
musket volley of round shot
even that aftermath ghosted and gone

THE SEVENTH MORNING

I used to wake early
on the seventh morning
knowing it would be
salmon sandwiches for lunch
after church
the farm kitchen
redolent with untinned fish
and the uncapped
sour pong of dill and green olives
with red pimento
you might suck from the centre
so the olive
resembled a wooden bead
from a broken necklace
cheap costume jewelry
for old women to wear
when they were
overdressed and widowed young
and there
with the wine-flavoured communion
still purpling the tongue
the unleavened wafer
a full-moon round and
flat as water-thickened paper

the gibbous host
swallowed in a lump
like something
you were sorry you had said
that memory
of wheat germ
gluten in a golden field
wind thistled in the thigh-high
harvest
praying against the scratch of it, praying
against rain crush
and ruined wicker
and bad weather
that browns the straw with work

all afternoon
those days, more slow-shadowed
than most
my father napped in bed
like the sick, like the sad
like the lonesome-for-company
elderly strangers dropping their heads
grown feckless in the heat
like under-watered houseplants

he would gather my sister
into his arms
saying to her, "what
will you do when I
am gone ...?"
and she would race away
weeping to her own room

and he would also
sing a song of dog death
a sad deep-voiced
chorus of "Old Shep" gone
tell stories
concerning the need
to shoot your loyal companion
the need
to put him down
among the nose-cold
pebbles and the common
grief of spades
then
that morbidity
closed its door and slept
in the hen-house quiet
of a pulled-blind bed

and I look back now
wishing I could bang away
at lost sunlight
strike it hard
like a big yellow drum
marching along on that farm linoleum
spanking yellow sky
like a giant Chinese gong
hammering it out to a bruised tune of thin brass
waking him up
like stage thunder
battering his door
like a Zulu shield
but his was ever an insufficient darkness
it was in him
and he wanted the night to stay

BRINGING THE FARMHOUSE DOWN

I remember
being in the old
three-story blond brick
Middlesex County century farm home
breaking the ribs of the house
sledging lath
the horsehair plaster
with continental maps papered
and falling away
from the walls
of the vacant room
I was a small boy
barely able to lift
the head of the hammer
pulling strong nails
with a crowbar
easing them out
the ghost dust of a gritty trowel
unbuilding inward
from the peen-bruise of the punched studs
and the dry-lime fragrance
of the splintering slats
breathing in white-tongued dust
all day tasting the mined earth
what born-in-bed generations
were billowing to the knee
our hands powder-white
roughened by work
and nicked red through dirt
like the scoring of errors
my palms

bubbled with blebs
that I dare not break

in the long hall
the wicker wheelchair
winced like a toy
while the girls played
broken-legged doll

and the sun measured
morning with a brilliant melt
like tall butter
until in the long-shadowed
wane of bent darkness
we set
what leans
against what remained
and walked to the ankles
in the wrecked world
our shoes going *grief grief*
in the sorrow shuffle
of a disorganized result

and we washed away
the milk swirl
of our labour
found our faces
under rinsed masks
setting the soap cakes
down smaller for that
in the decorative lave cradle
of the sink

"you were a strange boy"
my aunt
says of me now
as I'd said to her
at supper
"well, we'll never have
that day again …"
as a world-weary
nine-year-old it seems I knew
even then
there was a glass
I emptied
and one I filled
both from the same deep well
the drained glass always
heavy with a second thirst

WORKING THE LAND

in my mind's eye
I see it still
in the harrow dark of the day
the swath in the wake of my work
all shadow-damp
earth-toothed
and brown smooth
as brushed backwards nap
the line to the left
drying, to the left of that
drier, to the left of that—dried
the little ridges
reconfiguring
at the stump swerve

quieted like waves that find an island
to fade against
and then those green seasons
and after that, the oat force
of the grown-yellow field
in the bountiful whisper
of a drop-voiced heat
the fever breath and tall beard
of summer
then turning the grain
on the floor

the same dust that fell once, rising
ancestored
in the ghost grass
of old rivers
the humbled fertility
of the deep-ground dead
all cow-fat winters to come

and I am
remembering, how
long ago in my youth
bracing the mow
the barn groaned
like a great ship
tethered to the water-broken shores
of the world

my grandfather—gone, my father
gone, my uncle
gone—and the grief of it

slacking a sack in the wind

CRUSHER AND THE ASSASSIN'S HAND

our grade ten history teacher
the one we called *Crusher*
because of the way
he once
grabbed a lippy lad
by the shirt collar
lifting him a hand-span from the floor
running him to the back of the room
and slamming his body
against the wall
so he hung there a moment
and then slumped
into a moaning heap on the tile
an awkward spill
of gangly adolescence
as though from this we might infer

here endeth the first lesson

he'd also bloodied
Leonard Hearns's nose
for laughing too loud and too long
at a joke he'd been told
and then Crusher Clarke
seeing the crimson snooze
dripping through the boy's fingers
as though he'd suffered the spontaneous epistaxis
of an inbred Romanov prince

he said—"Go clean yourself ..."
and that was that

one time
a girl had failed
to complete her homework
and as was his habit
teacher walked the rows
looking for evidence
that we had answered all his questions
from the day before
and he stopped
glowering down at the blonde girl
her notebook blank but for what she'd copied
from the board
exhausted by math, she'd gone to bed

in a rage
he picked her up
desk and thigh
turned her
pockets to the ceiling
and dropped that clatter
so she crashed
and her broken binder
sprung its rings with a hard snap
and bit into her forearm
with a silver fang

and that was he
and these our schooldays
spent studying the moods of the world
at the coming on of war

and that was a year
I remember well

when he told us
the final cause of the first great war
the war to end all wars
the one my great-uncle Jack served in
the one where the mad poets lost their minds
and he told us
of that single cause
how one fine late-June morning
the assassin Gavrilo Princip
shot Archduke Ferdinand

thus setting in motion in a single month
all the bellicose armies of Europe

and now
as we approach the hundredth anniversary
of that event

I remain in awe
remembering
how we quivered in our desks
thirty obedient students
wondering what to believe

UNDRINKABLE BEER

for the weird hospitality
of my father
who was serving his son
undrinkable beer
from the skunk in the bottle
to the sludge
in the glass
it was easy to tell
that the brew
had gone bad
with the flat brown
swampy blur
of the liquid
where an undissolved lump
sank through amber
like fruit spoil
to the bottom
of a shaken jar
and the old man said
"I just bought it
 a day ago,"
though the date on the label
was ten years stale
and his mother asked
"George, why would you lie
 to the boy ...?"
and he sniffed
at the drink
as you would
at the rumour of gas
for fear you might die in the night

and still he refused
to reveal
his part in the bluff to himself
as I'm
pouring the ale down the drain
like the awful project of a naughty child
too old to be spanked
by a ghost

NAMELESS CHILDREN OF A LOST GARDEN

drawn by the sound of the sow's distress
for she was screaming
as though suffering
the agony and panic of slaughter
we two children raced
around the corner of the shed
and leapt up on the gate
stopping at the first slat
seeking an unobstructed view
for we were not yet tall enough
to see over the uppermost board
without the feel of the ache of the fence
in the sole of the foot

what we saw then
was a sow in heat
standing to the boar
in the barnyard
this event being
a most natural copulation
something from the breeding life

my farmer father
sheltered even his own daughter from
something the women at the house
must never witness

but you were a city girl
free as the wind
clearly fascinated
you pressed your body
into the broad ribs
of the gate, leaned in and over
and gawked—until
the boar stood down, briefly waving
his long raw corkscrew phallus
weeping a milky tear of his seed
into the earth
like old starlight touching the eye of a stranger

SWEET TOOTH

when my sister was a little girl
she used to sneak
into our parents' bedroom closet
where mother kept the humbugs
and she would steal
candy from the full sack
and sit there in the dark tickle
and the fragrance of mothballs and lilac
sucking on stolen confection
until the bag was empty
and flat as a dropped blouse

my father
would sit in church
tapping breath mints
onto his tongue
from a rattling pack
and there
in the third-hymn halitosis
his tongue whitening every quiet word
he almost sang

my uncle
loved horehound
the bittersweet mentholated
rock candy
brown as a bad tooth

my grandfather
loved peppermints
he'd keep a dozen
in his pocket
wrapped in a soiled handkerchief
and he'd pull them out
in white chain
clinging to the cloth
as though stuck there
by a dab of dry mucilage

in the front parlour of the farmhouse
three or four candy dishes sat
cinnamon hearts, gumdrops
jellybeans, and sometimes, the summer-melt of macaroons
handfuls of bad-for-you beauty
spilling their bounty on the maplewood table

so it should come
as no surprise to learn
that my aged mother her memory
clean as a school slate
should be caught
in the bellyache of evening
in the nursing home
having raided the cookie jar
and eaten up
all the ice-cream treats
she could find
refrigerated in the common room

how might you not smile
and think
poor dear—poor sweet darling

if your once-upon-a-time
colicky lad

should grow overfond of the past

THE FULL MEASURE

There's the voice of the dog in the barn
you can measure his mood
in the mind
take his size
from the weight of his breath
seek his span in the volume of sound
find fear in the blood
of his moon
or loss in his lonesome lament

you can know
both by girth of his ribs
and fall of his thought
how his heart
might break over hay
or race like a hare on the lee
where he's home
in the scattering clods
that scree
in the wake of his claws
what wags
on the hinge of a leaf
what sleeps
in a slow-dying snow
where the knots
are like stars
in his world
and the dust shafts
that swirl to be seen
seem angels gone mad
to the floor

what he names
for the car on the road
what he calls
to the yard in the dark
or the sun
if he's held until noon
is this not the shelter
of hope
is this not the lonesome
repair
come close to the lock

and I'll say
what's gathered away
in the windings
by rain and by wind
on the heel that covers the land

WHO WAS AUNTIE MCPHALE

she lay in bed
legless and silent
her hair pillow-feather white
her flesh white, limed white
her lips, a slack pink gape
taking in breath, mouth alive with gulps of air
like the small black well-hole of the mind
something to fall into dream-walking
the slow old oxygenation of her fate
with the sad rise and fall
of the counterpane over the sheet
like the waves of the sea
bleach-white where her blue hand-backs
rested and her dark pulse drums
like bird blink
she was bone-weak and weary
feckless, hen-voiced
wondering where went the girl of herself
where went the sister, the bride, the wife, the mother
the aunt—what youth imagines
of this regret is there
in the paling of painted stone
in the whitewashed windowless wall
when the barn on the grade groans
with harvest and the hay burns

the thrust in hand and the smoke makes a ghost
of the nail heads
and time's roof of midnight-blackened stars
falls to the floor
like red-watered rust in rain

THE OLD MAN'S HOUR

at the end
my father felt
mostly the fear of falling to
the unforgiving floor
and so we walked together
his hand
fogging my wrist
like a greying darkness
I could reach through
to find the weight of bone
the blue moment
the almost reified shadow
of his soul
and in that sadness
in that coming on
of the strength of sorrow
in the gown-gap
of his johnny shirt
and at what is now
become an old man's hour
let us call it
the ghost of woe
of each footstep's lamentation
in those slipper sounds
of a weak-hearted moving

what the oat pail wants
banged empty
what the water drum
wishes with the going still
of its shining meniscus
dulled by spill
in a dirt-dead field
where the stone boat
dragged all the dry thirst
of a long-forgotten day
where I'm once again weathered in sheep

and now, with father four years gone
his brother
sits tethered to a chair
his forehead port-stained
by knockout
in a hospital hall
his wrist
cracked in a cast

I'm left grieving the oak
in the otherwise empty clearing
that storm-trimmed
monumental wind-loss
that comes in the night
when we are not there
but dreaming

WILD MUSHROOMS

I did not trust my bachelor farmer uncle's knowledge
an expert of puffballs, mushrooms, and morels
though he was master
of the forest floor's
swamp-water spring
he'd park his truck
and cross the over-silvered
mirror of the ditch without a splash
then slog the algae-verdant mire
that broke its blanket
to a worn-through ankle green
to find the sacred hold
the faerie circle of his appetite
my mother's fragrant kitchen afterward
asizzle with the pan's perfume
macadam-black the full-pure midnight colour
of old and much-used motor oil
I would not eat the stuff
for toadstool's poisoned fear
though now I live in that regret

some say
the cities make us smart
where live the star-starved children
of neon nights
let's to the library
let's to the zoo
let's to the urban park
where squat trees thrive
let's to the cold cathedrals

with *this* worm in the font
there we built the madhouse
there we built the mall
there we built
the ash heaps of the poor
I see my uncle's knowledge
in his working hands
his gritty palms, the spore and gill
and now I thrill to know
the earth receives us
like the winking of a dusted eye
and we are rich with seeing
like the wind within these words
become the breath that bends the sun-gold wheat
this light, the light we all must sleep to dream

STAY

I watch him sit
bound to his chair
convicted of living too long
if he walks
he falls
if he falls, he breaks
like branches come down
at the graft
he's bruised with old fruit
he ripens
till he rots on the floor
like the storm-injured orchards
of autumn, he's
the snap-wristed man
his face

a port-stain where he's shaved
gone liverish yellow
with healing
one month with an egg
where the mind
used to furrow the field
and so
I watch him
tied to his chrome
lashed to his wheels
as he listens
to trees in the weather
give voice
to the wind
he listens
to rain giving language to glass
what sorrows the sun's
also grieving the stars
his heart's in a trap of the moon
gone slow
and the cruel nurse
Kindness says "stay."

THE INEXHAUSTIBLE POETRY OF DEATH

for Uncle John the dying shepherd

I sit beside your dying self
your breath soughing
in and out of your body
like a slow open-mouthed engine
four years before that
I'd been with you

in the eatery you'd called
the Peloponnesians
while you were ciphering something
with a pencil nub
on an open matchbook
with little room for the numbers
like a farmer doing the corn on pocket paper
and when I asked "what are you up to?"
you said, "I'm counting the days
until I'm one hundred"
and now in cruel November
a decade short of that temporal destination
you are lying on a bed
too short for your bones
arching your long legs under the sheets
and lacking the strength
in your curled hands
even to touch your own mouth
above white weave
you struggle to exhale
when the nurse inquires "how are you feeling?"
you say "insecure"

and in that sheep-count of hours
the old shepherd
with his crook of stars
comes strong to the dark
for the last child of that generation
born to the half door
of a roofless house
when the wolf leaps in with the rain

REMAINS

today
we dropped my uncle's ashes
in the ground

the sack straps lowered
like a cloth bag
formed into a bucket
for a well

the ready earth
received him
in its circle
like a post hole
augered on a farm

I thought of how
he feared
the empty hollow of the dark

this man
who loved all lambs
and like a child
caressed the wool
of one
brought to his bedroom
at the home

I want to say
that what we love
survives us
even as the shadow drops

to mark the leaf edge
of a sunlit tree

but someone said
our ashes are not ashes

no

we're mostly only powder
from the dust
of teeth and bones

THE THREE PHASES

first the baby boy
comes crawling
arm and hip
arm and hip
like a wide-shouldered pug
hands flat-slapping
the floor
spanking linoleum
with his open palms
making a purposeful impression
with the vaporous heat
vanishing in his wake
intent on *getting there*
feeling the joy
of movement
he stands   and comes on
strong, legs akimbo
like an old farmer
waddling, the furrow's hero, he rocks

as he steps and then steps
and then steps, then
he spies
The Times
left lying flat on the floor by his father
sits with a diaper-thump
like the sound of a sleeper
punching a pillow
he picks up the pen
holds it erect
a thin implement with the ramrod posture
of a military martinet
pushes the point
pretending to do
the crossword
not yet one year old, he
mimics his dad
puzzling the print
with black ink
"you doing the crossword,
buddy?"
his pop says
and the little lad looks up smiling
draws a crooked line
he's thinking outside of the box

THE FIRES OF TIME

my mother had a string of faux pearls
a plucky thread of them
she wore mostly to church
cheap costume pearls
good enough for farmwives
grown foolish only on Sunday
ajangle in plastic bracelets and black-heeled shoes, sun
shadowed
under blue-brimmed hats
dangerous with pins, in brocade dresses adorned
by breast-pocket butterfly broaches that rose and fell
on the breath
like petals on swells of the sea
she was lovely in lilac with
one fragrant waft at the snap of her purse
that clung to her gloves
like a coin in the lace
what spilled from the string when it broke
bead by bead
like dew swept from webs in the wind
what snapped like a summer's sweet pea
exploding in bursts to the floor
laying siege on the wainscot wall
or the dust gathered under the bed
where they candied the corners for years
like the seeds of a thousand-year tree
that wait for the fires of time
to open dark arms
to the sky

THE HONEYMOON SOUND OF THE PUCK ON THE BOARDS

on their honeymoon
my father took my mother to a standing-room-only
Red Wings hockey game where they perched
in the dark red-hearted heights
he in his wing tips
she in her brand-new stilettos
and she was Grace-Kelly beautiful
and he was handsome and slim
dapper with dark thick curly hair
and the big-car dreams of a farmer

and it was the winter of nineteen forty-nine
mild in January, the weather strange-warm
snowless and grass-soft as it was with the ways
of gentleness then
and the war was well over
with Howe on the ice, young and swift
while my mother suffered in silence
for her tight shoes
her unnecessary girdle
her pinched smile
soon enough, for love
she would learn
to stop singing, to refrain from dance
to no longer expect to go to the movies
to work in the kitchen
canning the apricot crop
to scald the jars
and pluck the steam-feathered hens
that lay headless and killed for the freezer

to wince at the sass
from a teenage daughter
to puzzle over numerators
with a son who understood
the art of a good quarrel
to lose a baby girl
only three hours old
and to live long enough
to be the eternally sad widow
turning photographs
to write the names on the back
just in case
someone should care

ELEGY FOR MY LOST SISTER

Janet Irene Lee, three hours old
February 18, 1956

my mother came home to the farm alone
to mourn the child she'd borne and lost
three hours old
already fading from her life
like milk stain from
an empty glass or colour
from a sunlit photograph

and every childhood year since then
I longed
to see her height mark
by the door, that measure made in mind
to dream how tall she'd be
how wise with books

how strong and lithe and beautiful
her blonde hair turning brown with time

and if I sought her in
a hiding place
in closet shade of cuff and hem
in crawl space waft of web
and scent of earth
or in the shadow wells
below the pine to wish her there within
a darkened sweep of fragrant shade

or if I called her
by her given name
the last companion of my boyhood heart
that breath might lift her briefly from the phrase
to say the gift of God we once received
returns and I am brother to one sister more
the one I lost as well when I was four

THE GRUDGE

My mother
is a very old woman
for whom
each passing moment
vanishes like evaporating water

the story
she tells most often these days
concerns the little girl
she once was
weeping in the classroom

an inconsolable toe-headed eight-year-old child
unable to say
why—that *Dell*
had placed a worm
in her brand-new closed-up pencil box
and she
could not say for the sobbing
she could only, much later
write in the margin
of her
grade-one reader
over and over and over
I hate Dell
and this loathing
has lasted eighty years
the thought
of that abhorrent earthworm
writhing in the fragrant darkness

lingering
in the marginalia

even now
she hates Dell, long dead *Dell*
she cannot abide
that awful boy

this grudge
the one she sharpened
pencils for
is what she remembers
and this book
she keeps by her chair

if it falls open—on almost
every page
the evidence repeats itself

and if you ask her, or even if you don't
she will gladly tell you
everything she knows
about the terrifying incident
the kindness of the teacher, the cruel
laughter of her classmates, the wickedness
of Dell, the little girl unable to catch her breath

as it is some nights now waking alone
in the nursing home darkness

THE THIRD KINDNESS

why do you say "I" so often
my aging mother asks—
her memory of morning blank as blue sky—
she accuses her talking son of the sin
of self-involvement
though he visits her frequently
taking the long drive
from his own lake house
following the coastline
among windmills looming like a shadow forest
pinwheeling dark lances
on the landscape near Lampman's cairn
past the Battle of the Longwoods memorial
and the old earthworks
of an ancient people
all shell circles

and ghost-stoned graves
making one green lamentation
for the coming on of summer
as this incarnation
of her vanishing memory
remembers one reprimand
for the son
whose voice she hears faintly
as if only
the third kindness
were true, the one where
you disappear little by little
from your own story

PAPERWHITE SIJO

the paperwhites are blooming for
Christmas with a honey-sweet fragrance
                    permeating the room
my elderly mother receives them
with a bland and meaningless smile
                         gifting her face
the dying memory of that vanishing
perfume goes into the darkness
                   like a second darkness not yet there

THE MEMORY ROOM

my mother dines now
in the memory room
she takes her meals
forgetful of herself in time
she eats well
and, according to the kindly
caregiver
is more compliant—
she seems to enjoy
the conversation
with the other ladies there
who likewise
have issues with recall

one woman in the geriatric hall
stops me
on my way away to ask
"where am I?" she inquires
"I am lost ..." she says
she seems a child
in a forest of shadow and noise
she sits there
locked within her night of mind
with everything darkening down
to one
ineluctable shade, there
in the moody fragrance of the old

she seems half-satisfied to hear
my meaningless reassurance

you are safe

and the sparrow in the feeder
watching the world
fat with seed
thinks perhaps
of a different
even more full-bosomed day
when being loved
was also and always
less than enough

SLEEPING WITH HER MOTHER'S ARM

she lies in bed
her mind
a broken-brain
companion
to her colder hand
she says
she's sleeping with
her mother's arm
it lay there
strangely shouldered
at her side
limp and warm
abandoned like the failure
of a lingering embrace
the lost caress gone still
that sweep of frozen fingers
like the ruin
of a dog-torn doll

she reaches
for and finds
familiar motion
at the elbow's inner crease
the cup and well
of flesh
within the bend
the delicate receptacle
the humerus and radius
receive
above the code
of the unloving wrist
such messages
so similar to tears
too dry to shed

her mother
somewhere in the world
elsewhere than here
her ulna ghosting
at the empty sleeve
her blue pulse
dreaming of an ever-distant heart

WHAT HAPPENS TO MEMORY

what happens to memory
my mother wonders
truly wanting to know
for she is
forgetting herself
in the cruel anesthesia of time

and we were talking, a few of us
in Moose Jaw
about time's arrow
my watch
two hours wrong
by the rhythms of sleeping
and waking
and dreaming of home two zones away

and he
is saying how wrong
we all are
for thinking in vectors
of the ineluctable
singing of the fletched
motion of the clock-watcher's life

think instead of the seasons
and also of the wheeling of stars
and the elliptical motion of moonlight
come summering through heaven
its white circumference
staining the sky
with its milky meniscus
of secondary light, stone light
light that dies in the water

how is it
in the skirt-gather
of the coming and going
on a shell-hushed shore of a far-off sea

we lapse
into faces
at a boy-shaved hour

or are heart-breasted
by the Kronos of bones
lactatory with new longing
with its blink of focused heat
blushing in the flesh
with a biological burn
at the locus of the body's desire in design

if the peach swells on the bough
and the rose blooms
in its bower
and the green meadow hums
like a lost hive
and the saw-edged night
strides in the mind
with its cloudy chorus of smouldering midges
adrift in the smoke-hunger of heaven
darkening down to the scorched wick
of an elm in the gloaming
thatched by the straw spoke of stars

and she is lost
in the unfamiliar repetition
of meals
where nothing the same is the same
while childhood oversizes everything
like a much-vined house
the windows gone green-blind in the glass
the eaves sagging on the sticky fingertips of ivy
rushing the roof new-shingled with leaves

how in the dark interior
of a stale parlour dusted in overgrowth
like a much-shaken mop
or in the dull sadness of a grey kitchen
gauzed by the web of a farmwife fading
she sees herself as mostly
the Mull child
the tow-haired daughter
of Lila and Harry
weeping all morning at school

MOTHS THAT DRINK THE TEARS OF SLEEPING BIRDS

my mother's memory hangs
on the lip
of a word
as though the sound of language
were blotting its ink
as it breathes
and goes backwards-black
to the blind-in-a-moment
blur of night
washing the colour away
from the world
like windows scrimmed
in dyed linen
that is indigo-dark to the hem
adrift on the sash
like smoke that smudges
lantern glass on a wick
foreshortened in fuel
that burned-off past

of blue gloaming gone grey
that deep-into-dusk
nocturne with its stilling of song
and voices gone loud on the lake
unavailable sun
unseeable moon
and the misty subsuming of stars

her mind
sees a butterfly
blue-winged on the wall
and she says
"I've never seen a blue butterfly,
have you?"

I tell her
... *there are many*
the swallowtail
the common blue morpho
the mission blue
the kainer blue
the blue crow, the blue pansy
and more ...

in Spanish I say
mariposa azul

in French
papillon bleu

speak in this meaningless way
to a woman I love
and was born to

I weep for the loss
without tears
the sob in my voice
concealed in sweet words

I've learned there are moths
that drink the tears
of sleeping birds

that lepidopteron thirst
in the rainforest dark
on the island Madagascar
while the magpie robins
dream of songs
they will sing in the dawn
moths slake
a desire they long to solve
in the salt wells of morphia

those moths
with no common name

those soft-winged thieves of weeping
stealing the sorrow of night

BECOMING THE STRANGER

in the residence, kind nurses
have taped the words
Irene's room
with an arrow to follow
on the wall
all along the hallway
a few dozen steps from the dining area
to my mother's open door

and still, I find her
wandering
in the wrong direction
searching, as though
lost in a labyrinth
and she is hopeless
calling out for help

exhausted
like an old child sobbing in tall corn
breathless
in darkness
at nightfall
in the autumn rattle
of a hundred-acre field
where the sky
comes cooling over the earth
and merciless moonlight
chills heaven
like the glancing of amber
in black water

when we sit
we two together
mother and son
with her photo albums
she turns
through pages
sweeping her hand
over once-loved faces
saying—I don't know
those people—meaning
her husband of fifty years
meaning her sisters, meaning her children
meaning her entire life
since nineteen forty-nine

she angers if we pause
to reflect on these strangers
then a snapshot of her long-dead
uncles falls free

and she names them all
at a flutter
as though she'd been
studying nothing
but the history of uncles
in candle-burn

and as she's vanished
she also comes clear

she is there
where the lost child lies down
waiting forever to be found

YOUR GOOD SON DREAMS

last night
I dreamed of my mother
blessed by dying
and though
I woke up weeping
I know there's truth in darkness
and cruelty in time
pernicious clocks mark out
her hours in relentless ennui
sun shadows blacken stone
like lichen lifeless in the light
and watches
count their water
count their granulated sand
slim-waisted moments
drift and blink
and monuments erode
like rain-rilled cliffs
that sometimes calve
let slip the rooted oak
the leaning pine
meanwhile the locust falls
against the voice of shade
and morning
sets an unfamiliar coast
and strangeness
at the shore
in shattered blue
made mutable with polished glass
and broken shells

WALKING MY DOG BY THE LAKE IN A LATE-WINTER RAIN

my little dog and I
are water dancing in wet weather
at end of winter on the beach
where snow rots off in heaps
stippled and filthy and basalt black and
marbled through with grey
cold and gauzy mutton-coloured meaty clogs of ice
congealed with thaw
become the ugly waxy ambergris of scored glass
the lakeside cliffs
weep into rain gather
from where the soaked hills hold
and there is a strange thrill
where streams lug silt
and storm spouts gush
rushing for the supersaturated green
that swells the surface off the shore
with buoyant volumes of abundant slush

oh my most ordinary soul
see *this*
and in *this* see
the all-too-often disregarded joy
that comes at hours
of overspill
confounded here and there
by hesitatious berms
the melt-off thinks its way
towards a shallowing
a fan-out like a liquid shell

my spirit moths my shoulders from within
though I am veiled with *thus and thus* ...
I want a body
to contain
what breaks, what shatters off, what fails
what fades, what lashes up
and dwells in stain
what strains to vanish even in
the widest eye
when all things dulled by time
wind up their clock hairs to a golden coil
of gratitude and grace

WIREWALKER

he set out
on the cable—walking
over Niagara Falls
as though balanced on a thread
in his electric-orange raiment
like a brilliant spider
on a silk
a lovely incandescent
Marbled Orbweaver
this Wallenda
a third-generation daredevil
slowing over the plumb weights
then quick
as an arachnid in a rush
from suddenly seeing itself being seen
in a busy garden
confident and striding
until he entered
the complex crosswinds

where vapours plumed and swirled
in a wet smoulder

it was then he felt
the breath and push
of unanticipated weather
it was then
he began
to pray to the God of sparrows
the God of gulls
and wind-hovering hawks
as he felt
the nudge and mischief
that does not love
defiance
and the ineluctable perils
that blur the burning thorax
of the wirewalker

his heart
and the drum-echo
of its pulse
blooming at the wrist with the flesh stung blue
the image of ancestors
the long drop of their dying
into the damp tear-gather of ghosts
the grey sorrow of rain pooling
in the long veins of an upcurled leaf
the thirsting lifeline
of a widow's palm

what morbid wishfulness
hushes in us all

though we're carried
by his brave motion
we also long in the deep plunge
of a common faith to go
roaring over the emerald edge
as we fall beyond knowing

SHADOWLESS

a ubiquity of sparrows
throngs the shrubbery outside my window
all of them flinching their necks
amongst green leaf-quiver
as they fidget
like bored children, and then suddenly
they all take flight
in an excited swarm
a fluttering host
of rain-dampened wings blurring the air
though they soon return
to the song-silence
of the feeder
seed-greedy and
hungering fat with autumn as it goes
thinning the wind towards winter
their small breasts
soft as the vein-webbed temples of an old man thinking

in the driveway, just beyond them
fallen apples crowd the gravel-busy earth
in unattended numbers, some hold to branches
red and round among the stink bugs
and coddling moths
that worm the crop to nothing worth keeping

how lonesome
each leaf seems in this grey weather
let loose and
drifting down
through shadowless light
with a delicate tracing of darkness

THE WAY IT MELTS AWAY, THE WAY IT STAYS

we walk in the false season
of cottonwood snow
the verdant
and tufted grass-pierced white
lays its downy drift on the world
like a worn-out bed
this late-in-the-spring
fecundity of weather
the old wind aches
with age
though the ground is everywhere
pin-feathered
like a killed bird
who knows
the reasons for the night
its reconfigured stars
breathing through this swirl and prick of light
the seeding
earth has lifted once more its
greensick garden
to the moonless dawn
that barely ever
remembers itself
under these

busy-as-an-anthill heavens
I hold my wife's hand
linger at the dog-squat
of an overfamiliar corner
where everything
is brand new
here in the cottonwood faith
where even the trees
believe in loving
the way it melts away
the way it stays

in the broken mirror
how many faces
are mine